Caught in a Hazy Dream

Contemporary Tanka Poetry

Tiffany Mackay

HORIZON
LITERARY HOUSE

Caught in a Hazy Dream

Contemporary Tanka Poetry

Tiffany Mackay

HORIZON
LITERARY HOUSE

HORIZON LITERARY HOUSE

Caught in a Hazy Dream Contemporary Tanka Poetry

Copyright © 2024 by Tiffany Mackay

Published by Horizon Literary House
First edition published in 2024

ISBN (paperback): 978-1-965285-04-6
ISBN (ebook): 978-1-965285-01-5
ISBN (hardcover): 978-1-965285-05-3

Cover design by Tiffany Mackay
www.tiffanylizmackay.com

www.horizonliteraryhouse.com

to those who pause
in life's rushing stream
to glimpse beauty—
may you lose yourself
in this hazy dream

Contents

Acknowledgements

Creating this collection has been a journey of the heart, and I could not have reached this point without the support and encouragement of many wonderful people.

To my husband and family whose unwavering belief in me fuels my creative spirit every day. Your love and support mean everything.

My sincere gratitude to the editors and publishers who have given my poems a home. Special thanks to *Humana Obscura, Cold Moon Journal, Plum Tree Tavern, Japan Society London Haiku Corner, Haikuniverse,* and *Scarlet Dragonfly.* Your recognition has been instrumental in my growth as a poet.

To the tanka masters whose work has inspired and guided me, your influence is woven through these pages.

Finally, to my readers who find resonance in these words— thank you for being part of this poetic journey. Your engagement brings these poems to life.

Poet's Note

The seeds of *Caught in a Hazy Dream* were planted during a particularly introspective period of my life. As I navigated personal challenges and transitions, I found myself increasingly drawn to the art of observation—noticing the subtle interplay of light and shadow, the whisper of wind through leaves, the fleeting expressions on loved ones' faces.

Tanka became my chosen form for these observations, not just for its brevity, but for its ability to capture the essence of a moment while hinting at deeper emotional undercurrents. Each poem in this collection represents a glimpse of my inner world, a frozen fragment of thought or feeling.

The process of creating these poems was often spontaneous. I'd find myself scribbling verses in pocket notebooks or tapping lines into my phone's note app while traveling. This organic approach allowed me to stay true to the immediacy of each moment, preserving its raw emotional impact.

Pairing each poem with digital watercolor art was a natural extension of this process. As a visual thinker, I often see my poems as color and form before they take shape in words. The abstract nature of these images reflects the fluid, often ambiguous nature of memory and emotion that I explore in my work.

As you move through these sections, I hope these poems serve as both mirrors and windows—reflecting your experiences and offering new perspectives. May they inspire you to pause and find poetry in your everyday moments.

Introduction

Welcome to *Caught in a Hazy Dream*, a collection of tanka-inspired poems that capture the fleeting beauty of life's moments. As you make your way through these pages, you will find yourself immersed between memory and imagination, nature and human experience, past and present.

This collection is divided into five themed sections: Misty Mornings, Sun-Dappled Days, Twilight Reflections, Starlit Journeys, and Dreamscape. Each section reflects a different aspect of the human journey—memory, love, growth, transformation, and the blurring of reality and dreams. Through these poems, I aim to highlight the extraordinary in the everyday, encouraging you to pause and appreciate the subtle beauty around us.

A Glimpse at the History

Tanka, an ancient form of Japanese poetry, has been cherished for centuries for its ability to distill complex emotions and observations into a few powerful lines. Originating in the 7th century, tanka has evolved over time, influencing and being influenced by the cultural contexts in which it is written.

Throughout history, many tanka masters have left their indelible mark on this poetic form. Legendary poets like Ono no Komachi and Izumi Shikibu from the Heian period (794-1185) created verses of profound beauty and emotion. In the modern era, poets such as Akiko Yosano revolutionized tanka with passionate, feminist themes.

Their work explores themes of love, nature, and the human condition, offering insights through simplicity.

In more contemporary times, poets like Machi Tawara and Takuboku Ishikawa have brought fresh perspectives to tanka, blending traditional elements with modern sensibilities. Their ability to capture the essence of fleeting moments with clarity and emotion has paved the way for a new generation of tanka poets.

A Contemporary Approach to Tanka

Inspired by history, my poetry seeks to honor the traditional form while embracing contemporary themes and settings. Tanka, with its five-line structure, allows for a nuanced expression of emotions and observations. While traditional Japanese tanka follows a 5-7-5-7-7 syllable pattern, I've chosen to break away from this strict structure in my work. This decision reflects what we often see today in contemporary English-language tanka, which tends to prioritize a moment or feeling over adherence to syllable counts.

Despite this departure from traditional form, my work remains true to the spirit of tanka—capturing profound moments in concise, verses. The fundamental rules of tanka still guide my writing: the turn or pivot that often occurs between the upper and lower parts of the poem, the focus on a single moment or emotion, and the use of natural imagery to reflect human experiences.

My approach could be described as freestyle or micro poetry, but it's deeply rooted in the tanka tradition. I've drawn inspiration from various tanka masters, particularly admiring Machi Tawara's ability to find poetry in everyday modern life and Akiko Yosano's passionate, emotive style.

Like these poets, I strive to blend the timeless aspects of tanka with contemporary experiences and observations.

Visual Poetry

Each poem in this collection is paired with an original digital watercolor background, reminiscent of haiga, the traditional Japanese art form that combines poetry with painting. These abstract, watercolor-like images serve as a bridge between the poetry and the emotions they evoke, adding an extra layer of depth and beauty to the reading experience.

I chose abstract digital watercolors for several reasons. Firstly, the fluid, dreamy quality of watercolors aligns perfectly with the collection's title and overall theme of being "caught in a hazy dream." Secondly, the abstract nature of the images allows them to be interpreted alongside the poems for a more personal experience. Lastly, the digital medium reflects the contemporary nature of this tanka collection, blending traditional inspirations with modern techniques.

As you read *Caught in a Hazy Dream*, my hope is that you find echoes of your own experiences within these verses. May you discover the wonder in the everyday, and let the words and images transport you to a place where reality and dreams intertwine. This collection is an invitation to pause, to observe, and to feel deeply—a celebration of the beauty and complexity of our everyday experiences through the lens of contemporary tanka.

Misty Mornings

Awakening to Memory

glittering stars dance
across the lake
as they did the night
of our first kiss
still leaving me breathless

dusty album pages—
faces I should remember
stare back at me
their eyes holding secrets
time has whispered away

sitting on father's shoulders
as fireworks mark the new year
I remember your laughter
how fleeting that moment
when the world felt complete

faded photograph—
my parents' young faces
holding me close
how strange to hold
a moment lost to time

the lemon tree is gone—
driving past my childhood home
a fleeting glimpse
of my former self waves hello
and goodbye at once

your hazel eyes
reflect the blue in your shirt—
my heart races
blinking—I return
to the thrill of our first spring

in the quiet park
our evening rendezvous—
the world disappears
together we envision
a future of shared dreams

looking up
I see the same supermoon
shining just like that night—
a different lifetime
when we watched its silver glow

summer downpour—
we flee for dry shelter
arms interlocked
our laughter bubbles up
drowning the rain

barefoot on the beach
sand sticking to my ankles—
memories of us
walking here together
laughter carried by the waves

walking by an old
sewing machine
I twist the ring you once wore—
recalling all the beauty
you created with your hands

sipping creamsicle kombucha
at the brewery—
suddenly I'm seven
racing down sun-baked streets
coins jingling in my pocket

handshake, photograph
tassel swings as I step off—
a vast future waits
yet in this moment of joy
absence echoes loudly

an old letter found
words faded but still so clear—
your voice fills my mind
telling tales of horse races
summer's golden memories

old coastal snapshots—
our sunburned faces
laughing at the camera
how light we were then
before we knew the weight of time

waist-deep in the sea
waves and memories surge—
sharp stones underfoot
anchor me to this moment
as past summers wash over

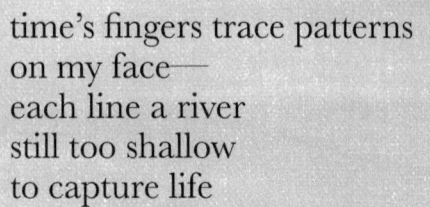

time's fingers trace patterns
on my face—
each line a river
still too shallow
to capture life

first summer heat wave—
uncapping the sunscreen
scent of last year's sun-kissed skin
coconut and laughter bubble up
like waves mixing with today

across the world
yet your presence lingers here—
"missing you" echoes
love's invisible threads
keeping us close

new finches chirp
welcoming summer's warmth—
in this strange house
we build a nest of moments
each day feeling more like home

Sun-Dappled Days

Love in Nature

oak's shadow falls
across my half-written page
knees touch
sparking a poem more profound
than words can capture

grocery store salad
shared on the picnic blanket
a bee's buzz startles
your lips curve upward
outshining the summer sun

soaking up
a season of summer
in a single hour—
each paddle's dip draws us deeper
into the moment together

red maples above
I stand alone yet not—
a crow's dark eyes
meet mine in understanding
nature's silent confidant

pine-scented air
the hustle and bustle fades
just us in this cabin
your presence fills my senses
more vividly than memories

the sun sinks slowly
behind the apartment block
golden honey spills
across my skin
summer's lingering kiss

lunch by the shore
sandwich half-eaten
kingfisher dives
ripples spread on water
mirroring my thoughts

golden sunset—
a bird's silhouette
cuts across the sky
in that fleeting moment
my heart takes flight

summer's embrace
we escape to the lake's cool kiss
splashing, phones forgotten
returning with joy
glowing on flushed skin

picnic in the park
trees sway above
summer's lullaby—
forgotten book on my chest
eyelids heavy with heat

scattered clouds
a bee buzzes at my window
pulling me from my thoughts
suddenly aware of
unread notifications

wilting roses
under the full sun
their fading beauty
catch my gaze
change is relentless

weekend getaway
oak after oak
sway on golden hills—
phone camera can't capture
how my heart fills with the view

chlorine-scented air
the dragonfly and bee land
in the pool—my shadow
falls across them
we're all trying to find relief

stubble on his cheek
a gentle, lingering kiss—
as we chop herbs
summer warmth slips in
through half-open blinds

yellow jacket and house finch
making their nests—
just like you and me
building our home
with shared dreams in these walls

sitting under dappled sunlight
we share an apple pie—
every bite a summer kiss
our love too
ripens each year

evening ritual
misting potted plants
cat watches from its perch
in our shared smiles
I see our future blooming

uphill struggle
heart heavy with doubt—
your hand reaches back
in its familiar roughness
I find the strength to go on

evening night breeze
crickets chirping
your hand warm in mine
under Orion's belt
time measured in heartbeats

Twilight Reflections

Self and Growth

towering red maple
when did it grow so tall?
looking back
I compare my growth
against its reaching branches

bare trees—
do they ever tire
of changing seasons?
such questions fade away
as spring buds unfurl

morning dew glistens
on unfurling petals—
window reflection
I glimpse my self
slowly blooming

spring rain taps softly—
in the mirror we face
fingers almost touching
as she reaches for me
hope in her eyes

evening's restless tide—
waves tumble pebbles and thoughts
on this lonely shore
clouds drift across the sky
hiding the silent moon

sleeping in—
winter blanket too heavy
restless legs
kicking free, I release
a tangle of thoughts

morning garden—
watering can tips over spilling
on the ground
my scattered thoughts
form in water droplets

wading into surf
thoughts swell like ocean waves
pulling me under
I tumble in currents
of my restless mind

mirage-like heatwave
shimmers on endless highway
roadside wildflowers blur
exit ramps curve away
into unknown fields

morning light spills
across the kitchen table
revealing old coffee rings—
today's mug breaks
the circular past

twilight deepens—
my shadow reaches past
the windowsill's edge
seeking purpose
in the world unknown

moths dancing
in the streetlight halo
the world fades to a whisper
stillness cloaks me
in summer night

morning light creeps
across cold floorboards
warming my bare feet
doubt retreats to shadows
in the corners of my mind

bathroom's harsh light
I tilt my head, searching
for that first grey hair—
new lines on my face instead
no filter can hide

autumn leaves gather
clinging to summer's warmth—
rake in hand, I pause
cool breeze whispers promises
of long, quiet nights

ripples on water—
above, two sparrows
weave twigs into home
I envy their sureness
in this changing world

lost in summer's haze
I blink—autumn surrounds me
fallen leaves whisper
their brown-edged reminder
seasons shift in a heartbeat

airplane overhead—
strangers fly to distant shores
while I stand rooted
watching possibilities
vanish beyond the horizon

bare lemon tree—
stark branches reach skyward
patient in stillness
I mirror its quiet hope
for bright days yet to bloom

nature's alarm clock—
sparrow's song filters through
the window
lingering dreams dissolve
as day sharpens into focus

Starlit Journeys

Travel and Transformation

end of summer—
boarding pass in hand
I step into the jet bridge
my story being written
with each uncertain step

California dreams
once distant as stars, now real—
I leap towards you
salt air fills my lungs
with courage for this journey

six years of sunsets—
collecting seashells and stories
from distant shores
our laughter echoes still
in the curve of each wave

under the Milky Way
we sail on moonlit waters
our voyage nears its end
on salt-kissed lips, we taste
bittersweet farewell

past falls away
like leaves in autumn wind—
I breathe in courage
each exhale carrying me
further into the unknown

autumn's last leaf quivers—
my heart, too, trembles
between known and unknown
yearning to fly free yet
aching for familiar soil

parting without promise—
nights stretch like an endless sea
between our hearts
I keep watch beneath
skies we once gazed together

novice surfer's folly—
salt and panic in my throat
until your steady hand
and laughing eyes remind me
why I brave these waters

jellyfish's sharp sting—
I flounder in doubt's deep waters
until your gaze
like a lifeline, pulls me
from the depths of my fears

beach-combing alone
I pocket smooth stones one for
each day you're at sea—
my collection grows heavy
without you

you dash ahead
around an unfamiliar bend
I quicken my footsteps
following blindly
guided by your laughter

endless summer—
golden reeds blur past
as we race the setting sun
each fleeting moment a brushstroke
painting memories in light

golden hills blur
into twilight—
our laughter echoes
across the fading sun
turning into dreams

city bus departs
my bag guards your empty seat—
the chill of your absence
turns golden leaves to brown
on this solitary journey

uneven on cobblestones
I adjust my backpack straps—
unfamiliar breeze carries scents
of local cafes, each step
more solid than the last

spring roll workshop—
clumsy fingers and laughter bubbling
between rice paper layers
crafting new friendships
lingering aftertaste

walking through the door
familiar floorboards creak
beneath my feet
past laughter echoes
in this silent welcome

trail fades
into misty peaks
on trembling legs
a loose stone tumbles
echoing my heartbeat

lost on foreign streets
comfort a distant memory—
each wrong turn reveals
parts of me long forgotten
hidden by life's routine

suspended in sky
fear grips me as plane wavers—
in your steady gaze
I find an anchor, stronger
than earth's lost gravity

Dreamscape

Blurring Realities

endless blue above
mountains melt to watercolors—
sun-warmed grass cradles
my drowsy thoughts, blurring
reality into hazy dreams

city lights blur
through rain-streaked window
it's your face I see
in each glistening droplet
past and present blur

early morning—
parting blinds reveal
a blanket of fog
cat stretches on windowsill
as world hits snooze

mist-covered mountains
vanish and reappear
from my searching gaze—
mirroring my heart
clarity just out of focus

drifting clouds above
carry my thoughts away—
in this moment
past and future blur
time loses its authority

summer's blazing days
I dream of autumn's soft light—
come winter's dark chill
my heart aches for spring's promise
eternally unsatisfied

stifling heat
thoughts heavy like summer air—
productivity
a mirage shimmering
just beyond reach

burning sunset
painting the world in gold
city and I on pause
silhouettes of birds
sweep across the sky

abandoning the shade
I brave the sun's embrace—
feeling the salty breeze
my worries dissolve
in breaking waves

lavender clouds
stretch across the fading blue—
concerns dissolve
in twilight's soft palette
hope blooming in pastel hues

heat shimmers
on sun-baked streets—
yet framed by trees
sunset's fiery palette
lightening the heart

end of summer—
the once vibrant blooms
bow their heads in surrender
I long for autumn's cool breeze
to sooth my withered soul

three becomes four—
night's heavy silence
as I toss and turn
childhood summers and deadlines
mingle in half-formed dreams

bird's morning song
pierces gossamer dreams—
half-lidded eyes
I grasp fading fragments
bargaining with dawn

sunlight warms my face
time slows to honey in this
golden afternoon
distant traffic's soft hum
measures lazy moments

winter's grip loosens
hope taps gently on
frosted windowpane—
I part heavy curtains to
welcome spring's promise

smoke-filled sky
sunset paints the world crimson—
beauty and danger
dance on the horizon
in an uneasy embrace

morning greets me
with spring's cool touch
while afternoon brings
summer's heat—I am caught
in nature's indecision

midnight stillness—
limbs heavy yet restless
mind adrift
reality and dreams merge
in the hush of the night

coffee shop chatter
mug warms my hands—
have I lived this moment?
sunlight stretches across the table
past and present blur as one

About

Tiffany Mackay is a poet from California specializing in contemporary tanka, haiku, and other short-form poetry. Her work explores themes of memory, love, nature, and self-discovery, capturing the beauty of fleeting moments.

An observer of the natural world and human experience, Tiffany draws inspiration from the seasonal changes and the interplay of light and shadow. Her poetry invites readers to pause and rediscover the profound in the ordinary, bridging the gap between the external world and inner emotional landscapes.

Follow her on Instagram and Threads: @tiffanymackaypoetry or connect with her on her website at www.tiffanylizmackay.com.

Tiffany's work has been featured in several publications, including *Humana Obscura, Cold Moon Journal, Plum Tree Tavern, Japan Society London Haiku Corner, Haikuniverse, Scarlet Dragonfly* and others.

Through her poetry, Tiffany aims to evoke feelings of peace and reflection, creating moments of contemplation that deeply resonate with her audience.

Her words invite readers to pause, breathe, and find beauty in the everyday.

Horizon Literary House

At Horizon Literary House, we are passionate about bringing contemporary micro poetry and prose to life. As a small, independent literary house, we are dedicated to discovering and nurturing poetic talent, providing a platform for unique voices to be heard.

Our mission is to create a community where poetry enthusiasts can connect, learn, and grow together. Horizon Literary House has ongoing submissions. To learn more about our submission guidelines, visit our website at www.horizonliteraryhouse.com and connect with us on social media: @horizonliteraryhouse.

By choosing books from independent publishers like Horizon Literary House, you're not just reading—you're supporting a diverse literary community.

Your purchase helps nurture new voices, preserve artistic integrity, and keep the world of literature fresh and varied. Every book you buy is a vote for creativity, innovation, and the future of indie publishing. Thank you for being a part of this journey.

Glossary

Tanka: A five-line Japanese poetic form typically following a 5-7-5-7-7 syllable pattern in its original language. Modern English tanka often adapt this structure while maintaining the form's essence of capturing a moment or emotion.

Haiku: A three-line Japanese poem traditionally focusing on a single moment in nature. Classical Japanese haiku follow a 5-7-5 syllable pattern, though modern English haiku often diverge from this.

Haiga: A style of Japanese art that combines a haiku or short poem with a complementary image, traditionally a brush painting. Modern haiga may use photography or digital art.

Micro Poetry: Very short poems, often under 10 lines, that convey a complete thought or image in minimal words.

Contemporary Tanka: Modern interpretations of tanka that may not strictly adhere to traditional syllable counts but maintain the spirit of the form, often addressing current themes and experiences.

Pivot: A technique in tanka where there's a shift in tone, subject, or perspective, typically between the third and fourth lines.

Kigo: A word or phrase that indicates a specific season in Japanese poetry, though less strictly applied in contemporary tanka.

www.ingramcontent.com/pod-product-compliance
Lightning Source LLC
Chambersburg PA
CBHW040903120626
46551CB00006B/624